SCHOLASTIC

Sight Word
Poetry Pag

**100 Fill-in-the-Blank Practice Pages That Help Kids
Really Learn the Top High-Frequency Words**

by Rozanne Lanczak Williams

New York • Toronto • London • Auckland • Sydney
New Delhi • Mexico City • Hong Kong • Buenos Aires

Teaching
Resources

This book is dedicated to my family.
-RLW

Cover and interior design by NEO Grafika
Cover and interior art by Jane Dippold

ISBN: 0-439-55438-1
Copyright © 2005 by Rozanne Lanczak Williams.
Published by Scholastic Inc.
All rights reserved.
Printed in the U.S.A.

6 7 8 9 10   40   13 12 11 10 09 08 07

Contents

Introduction 7

About Sight Words 8

Using This Book 9

Sight Word Poem	Focus Sight Word	Review Sight Words	Page
I See	**see**	a	13
In My Book	**the**	I, see	14
Colors	**a**	is, the	15
What Color?	**is**	a, an	16
I Can!	**I**	can	17
What Is It?	**it**	is	18
I Like	**like**	I	19
I Can Hop	**can**	I, like, a	20
I Like School	**to**	I, like	21
I Go	**go**	I, in	22
I Can Be Anything	**be**	I, can, a	23
Can You See Me?	**me**	can, you, see	24
I Have	**have**	I	25
Can You See a Rainbow?	**you**	can, see	26
Please Do!	**do**	the, your	27
I Am	**am**	I, a	28
What Am I?	**not**	I, am, a	29
Lots of Boxes	**of**	I, have, a	30
By the River	**by**	you, can, the	31
Mix the Soup!	**in**	the	32
Rain	**on**	the	33
Silly Rhymes	**look**	at, the, it, is, on	34

Sight Word Poem	Focus Sight Word	Review Sight Words	Page
What Can Fly?	yes	can, a, it, no	35
Good Helper	my	I, can	36
We're Going!	call	go, my	37
Here!	your	here, is	38
Happy Birthday!	are	here, too	39
I See This	this	I, see	40
One Little Blue Bird	little	in, the	41
The Wind Blows	wind	the	42
What Will the Weather Be?	will	it, be	43
What Do Kids Like?	we	like, to, do	44
What Day Is It?	day	it's, a, to	45
Please Come See	come	please, see, my	46
One Yummy Lunch	one	I, have	47
This and That	that	this, is, a, but	48
What Can You Find?	find	can, you, the	49
What Goes Together?	for	a	50
As Fast as a Cheetah	as	I, can, be, a	51
Which One?	or	a	52
Way Up High	way	I, see, the	53
Little Green Frog	went	the, little	54
The Bear Went Over the Mountain	over	the, went	55
Over There	there	on, the, is, little, over	56
Bugs!	two	there, are, on, the	57
Autumn Leaves	down	fall	58
On Halloween	out	the, come	59
Come On, Let's Go!	no	and, more	60
The Funny Man	had	there, was, a, he	61
My Puppy	and	My, can	62

Sight Word Poem	Focus Sight Word	Review Sight Words	Page
On the Farm	live	on, the, there	63
The Rooster	up	he, the	64
My Turtle	he	and, his	65
Can You Guess?	what	is, in, the, a, little	66
All About Spiders	all	are, have, do, yes	67
Who Am I ?	know	I, live, do, you, what, am	68
Say "Hello"!	say	I, can	69
Picnic	take	we, can, the	70
I Love the Earth	love	I, the	71
Everything, Everywhere	just	not, the	72
Monster Food	eat	some	73
So Many	many	there, are, so	74
What's New?	new	I, had	75
If You Ever	never	if, you, ever	76
All About Me	about	I, a, that	77
Things You Need	need	you	78
Where Is It From?	from	comes	79
Fuzzy Wuzzy	was	he, not	80
Animal Talk	said	the	81
Something About Me	something	there, is, about, me	82
If You Were a Bunny	would	if, you, were, do	83
Chocolate Chip Cookies	them	I	84
With You	with	I, will, you	85
Friendship Song	together	the, more, we, get, my, your	86
Friends	they	because, me	87
How Many	how	many, in, the	88
Parts of a Plant	has	a, that, what	89
We Like the Flower	flower	I, like, the, in	90

Sight Word Poem	Focus Sight Word	Review Sight Words	Page
Ten Little Dogs	**make**	I, can	91
Where, Oh Where?	**where**	his	92
How a Seed Grows	**some**	give, it	93
Go Get Some!	**get**	go, some	94
The Best Weather	**may**	it, be	95
Frog or Toad?	**which**	one, do	96
Then I Drew	**then**	I, a	97
At the Zoo	**these**	too, at, the, do, live	98
Make Time!	**time**	we, make, for	99
Mama Called	**called**	the	100
Where Could We Go?	**could**	we, go, the, to	101
My Little Hamster	**her**	I, give, that	102
Fruit Salad	**more**	is, so, we, can	103
What I Made	**made**	I, a	104
Where I Have Been	**been**	I, have, to, the, how, about, you	105
I Am Thankful	**each**	am, for, little	106
Another Word	**word**	another, for, is	107
Busy People	**people**	busy, in	108
Snakes	**their**	are, they	109
Bigger Than	**than**	I, am, a	110
When Is It Night?	**when**	the, is	111
Jump Into Summer!	**into**	jump	112

Introduction

Dear Teacher,

Welcome to *Sight Word Poetry Pages!* This valuable resource is a fun and lively collection of 100 reproducible, fill-in-the-blank poems, which teach and reinforce beginning readers' mastery of basic sight word vocabulary. The poems provide an opportunity for children to practice reading, writing, and spelling the words that appear most often in print.

On each page, you'll find a poem for one of 100 sight words. In addition to my original poems, I have included several of my favorite traditional or anonymous poems, selected carefully to complement the collection and tie in with popular primary themes. Use this book as a flexible resource to fit into your balanced literacy program!

In addition to the poems, this book includes:
- A handy table of contents listing titles, focus sight words, and review sight words for each poem
- Ways to extend learning
- Directions for creating poetry notebooks with children

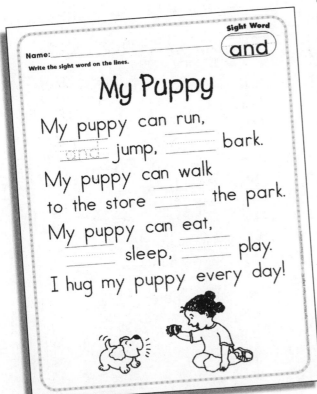

Name: _____
Write the sight word on the lines.

Sight Word
(and)

My Puppy

My puppy can run,
_____ jump, _____ bark.
My puppy can walk
to the store _____ the park.
My puppy can eat,
_____ sleep, _____ play.
I hug my puppy every day!

During my years as a classroom teacher, and through my experience working with, and writing for, beginning readers, I have witnessed the power of poetry in all its forms (chants, shared reading, songs, pocket chart activities, and so on) to inspire and motivate beginning readers. I hope these poems provide one more resource for you to build children's confidence—and fluency!

Best wishes!
Rozanne Lanczak Williams

About Sight Words

What Are Sight Words?

Sight words are high-frequency words—words that most commonly appear in the text of early readers. These words make up a core set of vocabulary that children need to learn in order to read quickly and automatically. Most school districts require that children learn to read and spell between 12 and 30 sight words in kindergarten and at least 100 in first grade. See pages 10 to12 for the Dolch Word List, a widely used list of sight words.

How Do Children Learn Sight Words?

Practice, practice, practice! A balanced literacy program includes many opportunities for children to encounter and practice sight word vocabulary. These words appear in the stories, books, and poems that children read, as well as in specific lessons, word-wall, and "word work" activities. These are words most commonly found in children's writing as well. As children encounter these frequently used words again and again, they will learn to recognize them anywhere without having to decode letter by letter.

How Will Using These Poems Help My Early Readers?

Learning to read, write, and spell sight words ensures the development of reading and writing fluency in beginning readers. The reproducible poems in this book invite children to learn, practice, write, and spell 100 basic sight words in the meaningful context of fun-to-read poems.

On each page, kids will encounter a new sight word in the upper right corner. Then the child has the opportunity to practice writing the new sight word several times by filling in three or more blanks to complete the poem. This unique, interactive feature provides valuable practice and leads to mastery of basic sight word vocabulary.

All the poems feature predictable, rhyming text and tie in with popular themes including weather, seasons, all about me, and more. Integrate reading across the curriculum with poems that have social studies or science themes. Use the poems in centers, add to poetry notebooks (see below), or create a supply of reading material for home. You can also encourage children to color the pictures with a variety of materials (watercolors, colored pencils, crayons, markers, and so on).

Using This Book

Introducing the Poems

Copy the page for each child. Before distributing, plan a way to introduce the poem, such as a shared reading activity. Write the poem on the overhead, chart paper, or pocket chart sentence strips. Write the focus sight word above the poem. Invite children to add the focus sight word to their individual word books, the class word wall, or their sight word card collection. (You might provide small file boxes in which to store cards with sight words or new vocabulary.)

After you've introduced the poem, children can complete their own poetry pages by writing the focus sight words in the blanks, then reading the poems on their own or with a buddy.

Making & Using Poetry Notebooks

You might invite children to create poetry notebooks that they can use all year. Each child will need a three-ring binder. Flexible binders are inexpensive and easy to find. Encourage children to decorate the covers of their poetry notebooks with their names, stickers, and designs.

These notebooks can build confidence and develop fluency in beginning readers. Completing the sight word poems, coloring and enhancing illustrations, and rereading the poems either alone or with a buddy make great center or free-time activities.

Use the sight word poems for other word work activities, also. For example, reread a poem together, and ask children to use a highlighting marker to mark the rhyming words, action words, or words with "magic e." One night a week, children can take their poetry notebooks home to read and share with family members.

Extending the Poetry Notebooks

Encourage children to write and illustrate their own poems to add to their notebooks. The basic sentence structure and repeated lines of many of the sight word poems make excellent writing frames. For example, children may enjoy writing their own "I See" (page 13) or "So Many" (page 74) poems. To keep the ideas and language flowing freely, keep reminding children that not every poem must rhyme. Share some non-rhyming poems with children and include them in your class poetry collections.

The Dolch 220 Basic Sight Words

a	because	clean
about	been	cold
after	before	come
again	best	could
all	better	cut
always	big	did
am	black	do
an	blue	does
and	both	done
any	bring	don't
are	brown	down
around	but	
as	buy	
ask	by	
at	call	
ate	came	
away	can	
be	carry	

Some of the sight words used in the poems are taken from other widely used word lists: The Dolch 95 Most Commonly Encountered Nouns, and the American Heritage High-Frequency Word List.

draw	help	may
drink	her	me
eat	here	much
eight	him	must
every	his	my
fall	hold	myself
far	hot	never
fast	how	new
find	hurt	no
first	I	not
five	if	now
fly	in	of
for	into	off
found	is	old
four	it	on
from	its	once
full	jump	one
funny	just	only
gave	keep	open
get	kind	or
give	know	our
go	laugh	out
goes	let	over
going	light	own
good	like	pick
got	little	play
green	live	please
grow	long	pretty
had	look	pull
has	made	put
have	make	ran
he	many	read

red	then	which
ride	there	white
right	these	who
round	they	why
run	think	will
said	this	wish
saw	those	with
say	three	work
see	to	would
seven	today	write
shall	together	yellow
she	too	yes
show	try	you
sing	two	your
sit	under	
six	up	
sleep	upon	
small	us	
so	use	
some	very	
soon	walk	
start	want	
stop	warm	
take	was	
tell	wash	
ten	we	
thank	well	
that	went	
the	were	
their	what	
them	when	
	where	

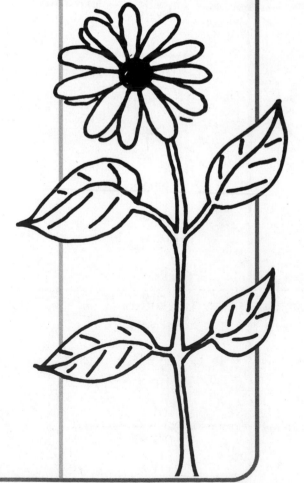

Name:_____

Write the sight word on the lines.

I See

I __see__ a cat.

I _____ a dog.

I _____ a turtle.

I _____ a frog.

I _____ a ladybug.

I _____ a bee.

I _____ a spider.

A spider sees me!

Draw a spider in the web.

Name: _____

Write the sight word on the lines.

In My Book

I see ___the___ apple.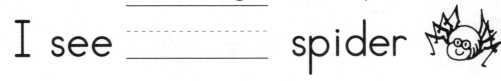

I see _____ ant.

I see _____ little bug

on _____ green plant.

I see _____ spider

in my book.

I see _____ turtle.

Have a look!

Write the sight word on the lines.

Colors

Orange is ___ carrot.

Yellow is ___ pear.

Green is the grass.

Brown is ___ bear.

Purple is ___ plum.

Blue is the sky.

Black is ___ funny hat.

Red is ___ cherry pie!

Name: _____

Write the sight word on the lines.

What Color?

An apple __is__ red.

A blueberry ____ blue.

A banana ____ yellow.

A lemon ____, too.

A carrot ____ orange.

An orange ____, too.

Fruits and vegetables

are good for you!

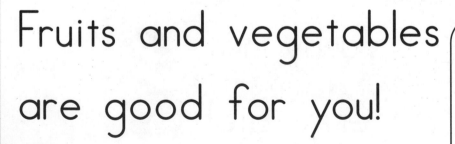

Draw your favorite fruit or vegetable here.

Write the sight word on the lines.

I Can!

I ___ can jump.

___ can run.

___ can play in the sun.

___ can swim.

___ can skate.

___ can bake a cake!

Draw yourself doing your favorite activity. Finish the sentence.

"I can _____!"

it

Name:_____

Write the sight word on the lines.

What Is It?

Is _it_ red?

Is ____ black,

with spots on its back?

Is ____ small?

Is ____ round?

Can ____ fly all around?

Is ____ a ladybug

I just found?

Draw a ladybug on the hand.

Name:_____

Write the sight word on the lines.

I Like

I __like__ candy.

I _____ cake.

I _____ the cookies

that I bake.

I _____ pizza.

I _____ popcorn, too.

I _____ spaghetti.

Do you _____ it, too?

Name:_____

Write the sight word on the lines.

I Can Hop

I _can_ hop like a frog.

I _____ swim like a fish.

I _____ look at a star.

I _____ make a wish!

I _____ hop like a bunny.

I _____ creep and leap.

I _____ go to bed.

I _____ fall asleep.

Good Night!

Name: _____

Write the sight word on the lines.

I Like School

I like _to_ read.

I like ____ write.

I like ____ share

and ____ be polite.

I like ____ paint.

I like ____ count. 1 2 3!

I like school, that's right!

Name:_____

Write the sight word on the lines.

I Go

I go in a bus.

I ____ in a car.

I ____ someplace near.

I ____ someplace far.

I ____ on a bike.

I ____ for a cone.

I ____, ____, ____.

Then I ____ home.

Name:_____

Write the sight word on the lines.

I Can Be Anything

I can _be_ a doctor.

I can _____ a teacher.

I can _____ a clown.

I can _____ a creature.

I can _____ a spider.

I can _____ a bee.

I can _____ anything

I want to _____!

Name: _____

Write the sight word on the lines.

Sight Word

me

Can You See Me?

Can you see _me_ ?

That's _____ near the tree.

Can you see _____ ?

That's _____ under the tree.

Can you see _____ ?

That's _____ in the tree.

Come up in the tree

and be with _____ !

Name:_____

Write the sight word on the lines.

I Have

I  two eyes.

I _____ one nose.

I _____ ten fingers.

I _____ ten toes.

I _____ two ears.

I _____ two feet, too.

I _____ one big smile

. . . just for you!

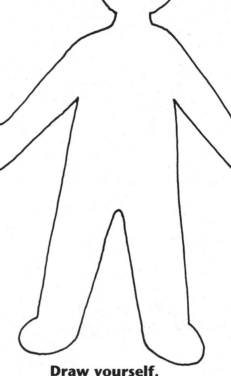

Draw yourself.

© 2005 Rozanne Williams

Name: _____

Write the sight word on the lines.

Can You See a Rainbow

Can ___you___ see red?

Can _____ see orange?

Can _____ see yellow,

green, blue, and purple?

Can _____ see colors

way up high?

Can _____ see a rainbow

in the sky?

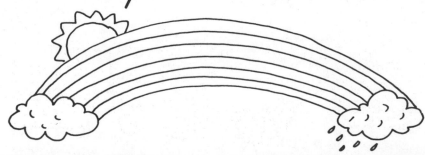

Please Do!

Please __do__ your homework.

Please sweep the floor.

Please _____ the dishes.

Please _____ your chores.

Saying, "please,"

is a good thing to _____.

It will help people _____

what you want them to _____!

Name:_____

Write the sight word on the lines.

I Am

I ___am___ a spider.

I _____ a fly.

I _____ a pretty butterfly.

I _____ a cat.

I _____ a dog.

I _____ a big, green,

jumping frog!

Name: _____

Write the sight word on the lines.

What Am I?

I am _not_ a cat.

I am _____ a dog.

I am _____ a spider.

I am _____ a frog.

I am _____ a fish.

I am _____ a slug.

What am I?

I am a bug!

Name: _____

Sight Word

of

Lots of Boxes

I have a box _of_ games.

I have a box _____ blocks.

I have a box _____ toys, too.

I have a box _____ paints.

I have a box _____ books.

But I have nothing to do!

Draw your favorite toy in the empty box.

Name: _____

Write the sight word on the lines.

By the River

You can sit __by__ the river,

and _____ the flower,

and _____ the tree.

You can sit _____ the river.

You can sit _____ me.

Draw yourself by the river.

Name:_____

Write the sight word on the lines.

Mix the Soup!

Mix _in_ the potatoes.

Mix ____ the peas.

Mix ____ the tomatoes,

if you please.

Mix ____ the corn.

Mix ____ the carrots.

M-m-m-m! Yummy soup!

Draw something else you would like to add to your soup.

Name:_____

Write the sight word on the lines.

Rain

Rain _on_ the green grass.

Rain ____ the tree.

Rain ____ the housetops,

but not ____ me!

Rain ____ the forest.

Rain ____ the sea.

Rain ____ the mountains,

but not ____ me!

Draw yourself under the umbrella.

Name: _____

Write the sight word on the lines.

Silly Rhymes

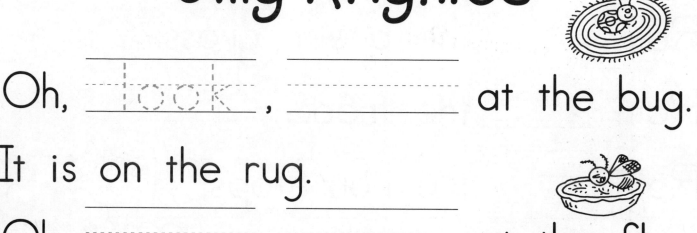

Oh, _____ look _____, _____ at the bug.

It is on the rug.

Oh, _____, _____ at the fly.

It is on the pie.

Oh, _____, _____ at the bee.

It is in the tree!

Now try your own!

Look, look at the _____.

It is on the _____.

Name: _____

Write the sight word on the lines.

What Can Fly?

Can a bee fly?

_____ _____ _____

yes , _____ , _____ .

Can a bird fly?

_____ _____

_____ , _____ , _____ .

Can a butterfly fly?

_____ _____

_____ , _____ , _____ .

Can a snail fly?

No, no, no!

It crawls along.

It's slow, slow, slow.

Sight Word

my

Write the sight word on the lines.

Good Helper

I can feed __my__ pet.

I can make _____ bed,

and put away _____ books,

after they have been read.

I can do _____ jobs

that I have to do.

I can be a good helper,

just like you!

Name:_____

Write the sight word on the lines.

We're Going!

Go _call_ my sister.

Go _____ my brother.

Go _____ my cousin.

Go _____ my mother.

Go _____ everyone

that I know.

We're going for ice cream.

Come on. Let's go!

Name:_____

Write the sight word on the lines.

Here!

Here is <u>your</u> lunch.

Here is _____ backpack.

Here is _____ jacket.

Here is _____ snack.

Here is _____ hug.

Here is _____ kiss.

Oh no! There is the bus

that you just missed!

Name:_____

Write the sight word on the lines.

Happy Birthday!

Here _are_ cupcakes.

Here _____ candles, too.

Here _____ balloons,

in red, green, and blue.

Here _____ snacks.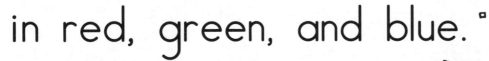

and goodie bags, too.

Here _____ presents.

Happy birthday to you!

Name: _____

Write the sight word on the lines.

I See This

I see _____this_____ frog.

I see _____ cat.

I see _____ bird.

I see _____ rat.

I see _____ mouse.

It is small.

I see _____ dog

who chases them all!

Name: _____

Write the sight word on the lines.

One Little Blue Bird

One _____ blue bird
sitting in a tree.

Two _____ yellow fish
swimming in the sea.

Three _____ orange crabs
crawling in the sand.

Four _____ brown worms
crawling in my hand!

Name:_____

Write the sight word on the lines.

The Wind Blows

The _wind_ blows the flowers.

The _____ blows the tree.

The _____ blows the leaves.

The _____ blows me!

Who-o-o-o-sh!

Draw flowers, leaves, and *you* blowing in the wind!

Name:_____

Write the sight word on the lines.

What Will the Weather Be?

Maybe it ___will___ be sunny. ☼

Maybe it _____ be rainy. ☁

Maybe it _____ be cloudy. ☁

Maybe it _____ be windy. 〰

Maybe it _____ be cold. ❄❄

What _____ the weather be today?

Draw the kind of weather you like best.

Name: _____

Write the sight word on the lines.

What Do Kids Like?

Do kids like to skate?

Yes, _____ do!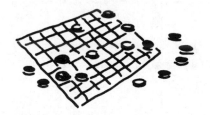

Do kids like to play?

Yes, _____ do!

Do kids like to swim

on a sunny day?

Yes, _____ do!

Do kids like soccer?

Yes, yes, yes! Yes _____ do!

Sight Word

day

Write the sight word on the lines.

What Day Is It?

It's a _day_ to sleep in.

It's a _____ to play.

It's a very special _____.

What _____ is it?

It's Saturday!

Draw something you like to do on Saturdays.

Name: _____

Write the sight word on the lines.

Please Come See

Please _come_ see my cat.

Please _____ see my dog.

Please _____ see my fish.

Please _____ see my frog.

Please _____ see my bird, too.

Please _____ see my pets.

Please take one home with you!

Draw a pet you would like to have.

Scholastic Teaching Resources *Sight Word Poetry Pages* page 46 · © 2005 Rozanne Williams

Name: _____

Write the sight word on the lines.

One Yummy Lunch

I have _____ one _____ sandwich.

I have _____ drink, too.

I have two cookies.

I'll give _____ to you.

I have some grapes.

I have _____ bunch.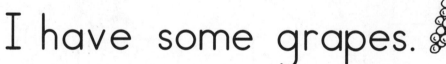

I have _____ big

and yummy lunch!

Draw your favorite lunch food.

Name:_____

Write the sight word on the lines.

This and That

This is a mouse,

but ___that___ is a rat.

This is a kitten,

but _____ is a cat.

This is a puppy,

but _____ is a dog.

This is a toad,

but _____ is a frog.

Write the sight word on the lines.

What Can You Find?

Can you _find_ the eggs?

Can you _____ all ten?

Can you _____ the mother hen?

Can you _____ the bees?

Can you _____ all five?

Can you _____ the bees

in the hive?

Name:_____

Write the sight word on the lines.

What Goes Together?

An apple ~~for~~ a teacher,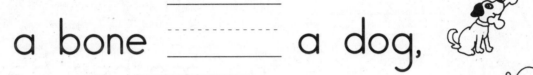

a bone _____ a dog,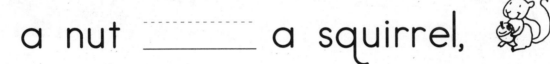

a nut _____ a squirrel,

a fly _____ a frog,

a mat _____ a cat,

a flower _____ a bee,

a worm _____ a bird,

a friend _____ me!

Name:_____

Write the sight word on the lines.

As Fast as a Cheetah

I can be  as fast

_____ a cheetah.

I can be _____ busy

_____ a bee.

I can be _____ slow

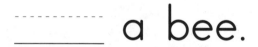

_____ a turtle.

I can be anything

I want to be!

**Draw an animal you
want to be like.**

Name:_____

Write the sight word on the lines.

Which One?

Which would you like for a pet?

a fish __or__ a turtle?

a cat _____ a dog?

a monkey _____ a zebra?

a lizard _____ a frog?

a snake _____ a spider?

a pig _____ a dinosaur?

Which would you like for a pet?

Name:_____

Write the sight word on the lines.

Way Up High

I see the black birds,

_____

way up high.

I see the white clouds,

_____

_____ up high.

I see the red kites,

_____

_____ up high.

_____

I can see _____ up

in the sky.

Name:_____

Write the sight word on the lines.

Little Green Frog

"Ribbit, ribbit!"

_____

went the little green frog.

"Ribbit, ribbit!"

_____

_____ the little green frog.

"Ribbit, ribbit!"

_____

_____ the little green frog.

Then he hopped

_____

and _____ over a log.

Write the sight word on the lines.

The Bear Went Over the Mountain

The bear went

_____

over the mountain.

The bear went

_____

_____ the mountain.

The bear went

_____

_____ the mountain,

to see what he could see.

Name:_____

Write the sight word on the lines.

Over There

Over ~~there~~ on the ground,

over _____ on the grass,

over _____ on the tree,

is something to see.

Over _____ on the ground,

over _____ on the grass,

over _____ on the tree,

is little me!

Name: _____

Write the sight word on the lines.

Bugs!

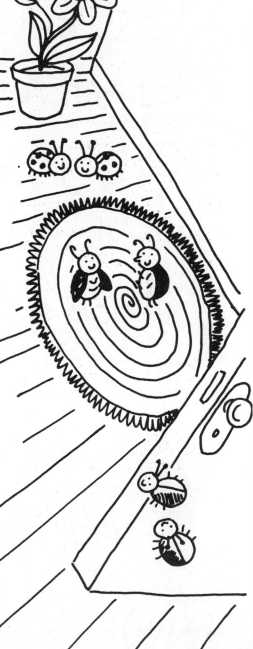

There are _two_ bugs

on the flower.

There are _____ bugs

on the floor.

There are _____ bugs

on the rug.

There are _____ bugs

on the door.

Name:_____

Write the sight word on the lines.

Autumn Leaves

Red leaves fall _down_.

Green leaves fall _____.

Orange leaves fall _____,

all over the town.

Yellow leaves fall _____.

Brown leaves fall _____.

Autumn leaves fall _____,

and cover the ground.

Color each leaf a different color: red, green, orange, yellow, and brown.

Name:_____

Write the sight word on the lines.

On Halloween

The bats come  ____out____ .

The cats come _____ .

The pumpkins come _____ , too.

The treats come _____ .

The ghosts come _____ .

It's Halloween! Boo!

Come On, Let's Go!

We have __no__ more milk,

and ____ more pickles,

and ____ more eggs,

and ____ more popsicles.

The answer to everything

is ____, ____, ____.

So we're going to the store.

Come on, let's go!

Sight Word

had

Write the sight word on the lines.

The Funny Man

There was a funny man

who _had_ a funny hat.

He _____ a funny dog.

He _____ a funny cat.

He _____ a funny fish.

He _____ a funny mouse.

They all lived together

in a funny little house.

Sight Word

and

My Puppy

My puppy can run,

and jump, _____ bark.

My puppy can walk

to the store _____ the park.

My puppy can eat,

_____ sleep, _____ play.

I hug my puppy every day!

Write the sight word on the lines.

On the Farm

Ducks _live_ on the farm.

Sheep _____ there, too.

Pigs _____ on the farm.

Horses _____ there, too.

Roosters _____ on the farm.

Cock-a-doodle-doo!

Cows _____ on the farm.

Moo! Moo! Moo!

Name: _____

Write the sight word on the lines.

The Rooster

He wakes ~~up~~ the cow.

He wakes _____ the pig.

He wakes _____ all the sheep.

He wakes _____ the ducks.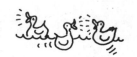

He wakes _____ the farmer,

and then goes back to sleep!

Name:_____

Write the sight word on the lines.

My Turtle

This is my turtle,

and _he_ lives in a shell.

And _____ likes his home very well.

See, _____ pokes his head out

when _____ wants to eat,

and _____ pulls it back in

when _____ wants to sleep!

Write the sight word on the lines.

Can You Guess?

Guess ~~what~~ is in the log.

_____ is it?

A little frog.

Guess _____ is in the tree.

_____ is it?

A little bee.

Guess _____ is in the box.

_____ is it?

A little fox.

Name:_____

Write the sight word on the lines.

All About Spiders

Are ___all___ spiders arachnids?

Do _____ spiders have 8 legs?

Do they _____ have 2 body parts?

Do they _____ hatch from eggs?

Yes, _____ spiders are arachnids.

Yes, _____ spiders have 8 legs.

Yes, they _____ have 2 body parts.

Yes, they _____ hatch from eggs.

Name:_____

Write the sight word on the lines.

Who Am I?

I live in the ocean.

I swim and I swish.

Do you ___know___ what I am?

Do you _____, do you _____?

I am a fish.

I can live anywhere.

I crawl under rugs.

Do you _____ what I am?

Do you _____, do you _____?

I am a bug.

Name:_____

Write the sight word on the lines.

Say "Hello!"

I can _say_, "Hola!"

"Bonjour!" "Hello!"

I can _____ it fast.

I can _____ it slow.

I can _____, "Guten Tag!"

"Buon Giorno!" "Good Day!"

I can _____ hello to you

in so many ways!

Name:_____

Write the sight word on the lines.

Picnic

We can _take_ the sandwiches.

We can _____ the pies.

We can _____ the drinks,

but not the flies!

We can _____ the apples.

We can _____ the tomatoes.

We can _____ the tacos,

but not the mosquitoes!

Name:_____

Write the sight word on the lines.

I Love the Earth

I ~~love~~ the flowers.

I _____ the trees.

I _____ the animals,

and the fish in the seas.

I _____ the desert,

and the rain forest, too.

I _____ the Earth.

It's home for me and you.

Name:_____

Write the sight word on the lines.

Everything, Everywhere

Not ~~just~~ the rivers.

Not _____ the seas.

Not _____ the flowers.

Not _____ the trees.

Not _____ the animals.

Not _____ the air.

Take care of everything,

everywhere!

Name:_____

Write the sight word on the lines.

Monster Food

Some monsters __eat__ pie.

Some monsters _____ rice.

Some monsters _____ pizza.

Some monsters _____ mice!

Some monsters _____ spiders.

Some monsters _____ bugs.

Some monsters _____ worms.

Some monsters _____ slugs!

Draw some monster food on the plates!

Name:_____

Write the sight word on the lines.

So Many

There are so ___many___ stars.

There are so _____ trees.

There are so _____ flowers.

But there is only one me.

There are so _____ fish

in the deep blue sea.

There are so _____ things,

but there is only one me!

new

Write the sight word on the lines.

What's New?

I had _new_ socks.

I had _____ shoes.

I had a _____ t-shirt,

and my shorts were _____, too.

I had all _____ clothes,

and a _____ belt too—

'til I fell in the mud

and got covered in goo!

If You Ever

If you ever

meet a whale,

_____

you must __never__ touch its tail.

For if you ever

touch its tail,

_____ _____

you will _____, _____,

_____ _____

_____, _____,

meet another whale.

Name:_____

Write the sight word on the lines.

All About Me

I wrote a story.

_____

It is all _about_ me:

_____

_____ things that I do,

_____ things that I see.

I wrote _____ friends

and my family.

I wrote _____ everything—

all _____ me.

Name:_____

Write the sight word on the lines.

Things You Need

You ___need___ food to eat.

You _____ water to drink.

You _____ a home.

You _____ love.

That's what I think!

Sight Word

from

Write the sight word on the lines.

Where Is It From?

Bread comes <u>from</u> wheat.

Apples come _____ trees.

Milk comes _____ cows.

Honey comes _____ bees.

Name:_____

Write the sight word on the lines.

Fuzzy Wuzzy

Fuzzy Wuzzy _was_ a bear.

Fuzzy Wuzzy had no hair.

Fuzzy Wuzzy _____ not fuzzy,

_____ he?

No, he _____ not!

Name:_____

Write the sight word on the lines.

Animal Talk

"Bow-wow," said the dog.

"Meow," _____ the cat.

"Oink, oink," _____ the pig.

"Quack, quack," _____ the duck.

"Who, who," _____ the owl.

"Chirp, chirp," _____ the bird.

"Moo, moo," _____ the cow.

"QUIET!" _____ the sleepy farmer.

Name: _____

Write the sight word on the lines.

Something About Me

There is _something_ about me,

it is _____ I know.

There is _____ about me,

but it does not show.

There is _____ about me,

I can grow!

Name:_____

Write the sight word on the lines.

If You Were a Bunny

If you were a bunny,

what _would_ you do?

If I were a bunny,

here's what I _____ do:

I _____ hop, hop, hop.

I _____ flip and flop.

I _____ never stop!

Name:_____

Write the sight word on the lines.

Chocolate Chip Cookies

I make ___them___ .

I bake _____ .

I munch _____ .

I crunch _____ .

I love _____ !

I want more of _____ !

They're pretty good stuff.

I can't get enough.

Chocolate chip cookies!

Name:_____

Write the sight word on the lines.

With You

I will run <u>with</u> you.

I will play _____ you.

I will read _____ you,

and ride bikes _____ you.

I will be _____ you

to the very end,

all because I am a friend!

Name:_____

Write the sight word on the lines.

Friendship Song

The more we get _together_ ,

_____

_____ , _____ ,

_____

the more we get _____ ,

the happier we'll be.

'Cause your friends

are my friends,

and my friends

are your friends.

The more we get _____ ,

the happier we'll be.

Friends

I like friends. Ask me why.

Because they help me.

Because _____ share with me.

Because _____ play with me.

Because _____ tell me jokes.

That is why I like friends!

Name:_____

Write the sight word on the lines.

How Many

Count ___how___ many bunnies.

Count _____ many bees.

Count _____ many birds

are sitting in the tree.

Count _____ many ladybugs,

_____ many in all?

Count _____ many frogs

are sitting on the wall.

Name:_____

Write the sight word on the lines.

Parts of a Plant

A plant __has__ roots.

A plant _____ a stem.

And it _____ leaves that grow.

A plant _____ flowers.

A plant _____ seeds.

This is what I know.

Name: _____

Write the sight word on the lines.

flower

We Like the Flower

"I like the 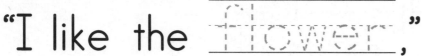,"

said the yellow bumblebee.

"I like the ,"

said the bird in the tree.

"I like the ,"

said the man in the sun.

"We all like the ,"

said everyone!

Name:_____

Write the sight word on the lines.

Ten Little Dogs

I have ten little dogs,

and they belong to me.

I can _make_ them do tricks.

Do you want to see?

I can _____ them jump high,

and _____ them jump low.

I can _____ them roll over,

and sit just so.

Write the sight word on the lines.

Where, Oh Where?

Oh where, oh _____

has my little dog gone?

Oh _____, oh _____

can he be?

With his tail cut short

and his ears cut long.

Oh _____, oh _____ is he?

Name:_____

Write the sight word on the lines.

How a Seed Grows

Give it _some_ soil.

Give it _____ air.

Give it _____ water,

time, and care.

Give it _____ sunshine,

and what do you know!

Soon the seed will start

to grow.

Name:_____

Write the sight word on the lines.

Go Get Some!

Go _get_ some pizza.

Go _____ some crackers.

Go _____ some cookies.

Go _____ some snackers.

Go _____ some ice cream.

Go _____ some cake.

Go _____ a doctor.

I have a tummy ache!

Name: _____

Write the sight word on the lines.

The Best Weather

It ___may___ be hot

or cold outside.

It _____ be rainy, too.

It _____ be windy.

It _____ be snowy.

What's the best weather

for you?

Name:_____

Write the sight word on the lines.

Frog or Toad?

Do you know _which_ is slimy

and smooth, wet and thin,

and _____ one is warty

with rough and dry skin?

Which one is _____?

It's hard to be sure.

But neither one barks,

and neither one purrs.

Frog

Toad

Name:_____

Write the sight word on the lines.

Then I Drew

First I drew the grass.

And ~~then~~ I drew a tree.

And _____ I drew a flower.

And _____ I drew me!

And _____ I drew a sun.

I drew a cloud, too.

I drew a pretty picture—

just for you!

At the Zoo

Lions, tigers, elephants too.

Do _these_ animals live at the zoo?

Monkeys, chimpanzees, kangaroos.

Do _____ animals live at the zoo?

Zebras, giraffes, penguins too.

Do _____ animals live at the zoo?

Yes, they do!

Name:_____

Write the sight word on the lines.

Make Time!

We make ~~time~~ for breakfast.

We make _____ for lunch.

We make _____ for dinner,

and for snacks to munch.

We make _____ for work.

We make _____ for play.

We make _____ for everything,

each and every day!

Write the sight word on the lines.

Mama Called

Mama ___called___ the doctor.

Mama _____ the nurse.

Mama _____ the lady

with the alligator purse.

Mama _____ the sleepy child.

She _____, "Hey you sleepyhead!"

Mama _____ and called

to get me out of bed.

Name:_____

Write the sight word on the lines.

Where Could We Go?

We _could_ go the desert.

We _____ go to the sea.

We _____ go to the Arctic.

We _____ go and see.

We _____ see mountains.

We _____ have a look.

We _____ go anywhere

. . . if we read a book!

Name:_____

Write the sight word on the lines.

My Little Hamster

I give ___her___ water.

I give _____ seeds.

I give _____ anything

  that she needs.

I give _____ head a little pat.

I love my hamster,

  and that is that.

Name:_____

Write the sight word on the lines.

Fruit Salad

Add _more_ strawberries.

Add _____ grapes.

Add _____ bananas.

Fruit salad is great!

Add _____ peaches.

Add _____ pears.

Add _____ apples,

so we can share!

Name:_____

made

Write the sight word on the lines.

What I Made

I _made_ a cake.

I _____ cookies, too.

I _____ a picture,

with lots of glue.

What else did I make?

Can you guess?

Oh no!

I _____ a big, big mess.

Name:_____

Write the sight word on the lines.

Where I Have Been

I have ___been___ to the farm.

I have _____ to the zoo.

I have _____ to the park.

How about you?

I have _____ to the ocean,

and the county fair, too.

I have _____ to the museum.

How about you?

Draw a place you have been.

Name:_____

Write the sight word on the lines.

each

I Am Thankful

I am thankful. . .

for _____each_____ little raindrop,

for _____ little stone,

for _____ little leaf on a tree,

for _____ little flower,

for _____ little bug,

and I am thankful for you and me!

Draw something you are thankful for.

Name:_____

Write the sight word on the lines.

Another Word

Another ~~word~~ for friend

is pal.

Another _____ for dog

is pup.

Another _____ for cat

is kitty.

Another _____ for mug

is cup.

Name:_____

Write the sight word on the lines.

people

Busy People

Busy _people_ in buses,

busy _____ in trains,

busy _____ in taxis,

rushing to catch planes.

Busy _____ in buildings,

busy _____ on stairs.

Busy _____ in the city

are everywhere!

Write the sight word on the lines.

Snakes

Snakes' bodies are long,

and ~~their~~ heads are small.

They don't have any legs at all—

_____ skin is smooth,

_____ eyes are round.

They slither _____ bellies

along the ground.

Name:_____

Write the sight word on the lines.

Bigger Than

I am bigger ~~than~~ a goldfish,

or a little snail's house.

I am bigger _____ a bug or ant.

I am a little mouse.

I am bigger _____ an elephant,

or maybe two or three.

I am bigger _____ any animal.

I am a blue whale in the sea!

Name:_____

Write the sight word on the lines.

When Is It Night?

It is night. . .

_____ **when** the sun goes down,

_____ the stars come out,

_____ owls and raccoons

are up and about,

_____ I go to bed,

_____ the moon is bright,

_____ the crickets chirp,

then it is night.

Jump Into Summer!

Jump _into_ sunshine.

Jump _____ shade.

Jump _____ ice cream

and cold lemonade.

Jump _____ the pool.

Don't be the last one.

Jump _____ summer.

Summer is fun!